North American
INDIAN NATIONS

NATIVE PEOPLES
of the
NORTHEAST

Liz Sonneborn

LERNER PUBLICATIONS ◆ MINNEAPOLIS

The editors would like to note that we have made every effort to work with consultants from various nations, as well as fact-checkers, to ensure that the content in this series is accurate and appropriate. In addition to this title, we encourage readers to seek out content produced by the nations themselves online and in print.

Consultants: Dr. Jill Doerfler, associate professor, American Indian Studies, University of Minnesota–Duluth (White Earth Anishinaabe); Jim Rementer, Director, Lenape Language Project of the Delaware Tribe (Lenape/Delaware)

Lerner Publications Company
A division of Lerner Publishing Group, Inc.
241 First Avenue North
Minneapolis, MN 55401 USA

For reading levels and more information, look up this title at www.lernerbooks.com.

Main body text set in Rockwell Std Light 12/16.
Typeface provided by Monotype Typography.

Library of Congress Cataloging-in-Publication Data

Sonneborn, Liz.
    Native peoples of the Northeast / Liz Sonneborn.
        pages cm. — (North American Indian nations)
    Audience: Grades 4–6.
    ISBN 978-1-4677-7933-3 (lb : alk. paper) — ISBN 978-1-4677-8323-1 (pb : alk. paper) — ISBN 978-1-4677-8324-8 (.pdf)
    1. Indians of North America—Northeastern States—Juvenile literature. I. Title.
E78.E2S58 2014
974—dc23   2014038436

Manufactured in the United States of America
1 – PC – 7/15/16

CONTENTS

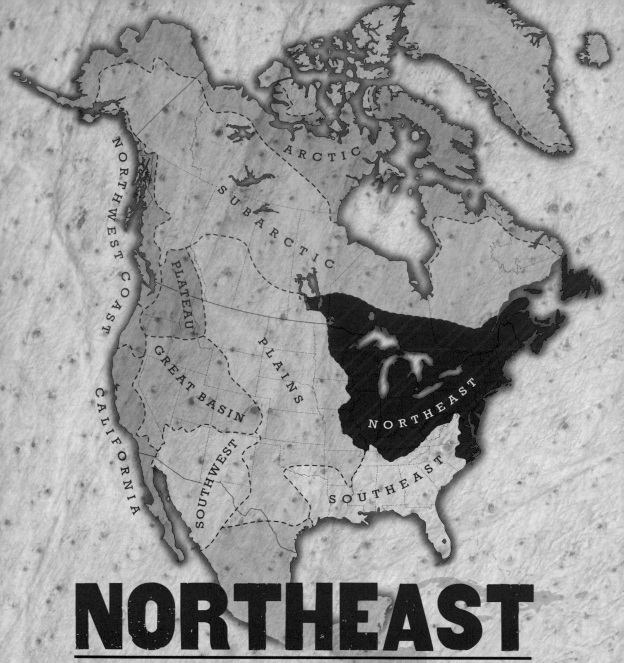

NORTHEAST
REGION OF NORTH AMERICA

CULTURAL REGIONS OF THE UNITED STATES AND CANADA

- Plateau
- Northwest Coast
- California
- Plains
- Southeast
- Southwest
- Great Basin
- Northeast
- Subarctic
- Arctic
- Other

- - - Cultural area border
- —— International border
- ········ State/province border

INTRODUCTION

Sky Woman tumbled through a hole in the sky. An endless sea lay below her. Animals in the water watched Sky Woman fall. Then a huge turtle came to the surface. Sky Woman landed safely on the turtle's shell.

The animals decided to make a world for Sky Woman to live on. A duck dove into the water to bring up mud. He died. A small fish dove next, but he also died. Finally, a muskrat took his turn. He brought up mud and smeared it on the turtle's back. From the mud, the world grew.

The Seneca (SEN-uh-kah) Indians have long told this story of how the world was created. It is one of many very old stories of the American Indians of the Northeast. The Northeast includes much of the present-day eastern United States and parts of southeastern Canada.

Many scholars believe people first settled in North America about twenty thousand years ago. These people may have crossed a land bridge from Asia. They were the ancestors of modern American Indians, including the native peoples of the Northeast. However, Northeast Indians tell different stories about their beginnings, such as the story of Sky Woman. These stories have been passed down through many generations.

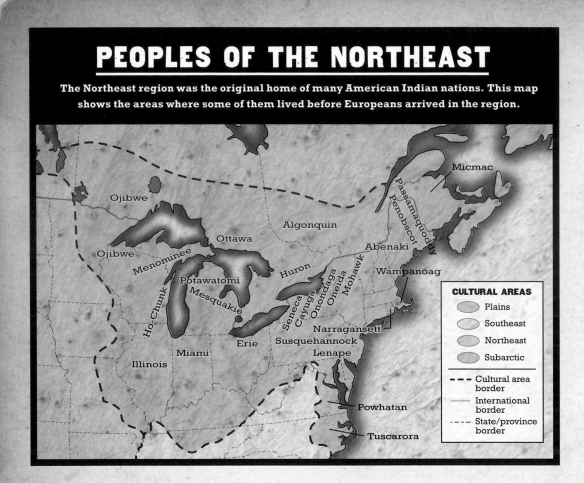

PEOPLES OF THE NORTHEAST

The Northeast region was the original home of many American Indian nations. This map shows the areas where some of them lived before Europeans arrived in the region.

Micmac

Ojibwe

Passamaquoddy
Penobscot

Algonquin

Ottawa

Ojibwe

Menominee

Abenaki

Huron

Wampanoag

Potawatomi

Mesquakie

Ho-Chunk

Seneca
Cayuga
Onondaga
Oneida
Mohawk

CULTURAL AREAS

Plains

Southeast

Northeast

Subarctic

Narragansett

Erie

Susquehannock

Miami

Lenape

Illinois

- - - Cultural area border

International border

-·-·- State/province border

Powhatan

Tuscarora

Many Nations

Around 1500, Europeans began writing about the people they met on the coast of North America. By then many separate American Indian nations existed in the Northeast. Each nation had its own identity, system of government, and way of life. But the nations of the Northeast also had much in common.

Northeast Indians speak languages from three different language families—Algonquian (al-GON-kee-an), Iroquoian (ear-oh-KWOY-ee-an), and Siouan (SOO-an). Each language family includes many different but related languages. Nations that belong to the same language family share many cultural traits in addition to similar languages.

Algonquian-speaking peoples were spread throughout the region. They got much of their food by farming. They also fished, hunted, and gathered wild plants. Algonquians lived in small bands and moved frequently. The Menominee (meh-NOM-uh-nee) and Potawatomi (pah-toe-WAH-toe-mee) lived along the Great Lakes. The Algonquin (al-GON-kin) and the Ottawa (AH-tuh-wuh) lived in present-day Canada. The Abenaki (AB-eh-na-kee), Lenape (len-AHPE), Wampanoag (wam-puh-NO-ag), and Narragansett (nahr-ruh-GAN-sit) made their homes in areas that later became New England states. To the south, members of the Powhatan (POW-ah-tan or pow-HAH-tan) Confederacy lived in present-day Virginia.

The Northeast region was rich in resources. Many areas were covered in forests.

LANGUAGE FAMILIES OF NORTHEAST PEOPLES

LANGUAGE FAMILY	MAJOR PEOPLES
Algonquian	Abenaki, Algonquin, Illinois, Kickapoo, Lenape, Mahican, Malecite, Menominee, Mesquakie (also called Fox), Miami, Micmac, Mohegan, Narragansett, Ojibwe, Ottawa, Passamaquoddy, Penobscot, Pequot, Potawatomi, Powhatan Confederacy, Wampanoag
Iroquoian	Cayuga, Erie, Huron, Mohawk, Neutral, Oneida, Onondaga, Seneca, Susquehannock, Tuscarora
Siouan	Ho-Chunk (also called Winnebago)

Iroquoian-speaking peoples mostly lived near Lake Erie and Lake Ontario. Like Algonquians, Iroquoians hunted animals and gathered plants. But much more of their food came from farming. Iroquoian peoples spent most of the year in large permanent villages near their crop fields. Some Iroquoian peoples, such as the Huron (HYUR-on) and Neutral (NOO-tral), lived in present-day Canada. Others, such as the Tuscarora (tusk-uh-ROAR-uh), lived in parts of what became North Carolina and Virginia. Many others lived in present-day Delaware, New York, and Pennsylvania. These included the Mohawk (MO-hawk), Oneida (oh-NIE-duh), Onondaga (on-uhn-DAH-guh), Cayuga (kay-OO-guh), Seneca, Erie (EAR-ee), and Susquehannock (sus-kwuh-HAN-ock).

Siouan-speaking peoples lived on the western edge of the region. In the 1500s and 1600s, most of them moved even farther west to the Great Plains. Only the Ho-Chunk (HOH-chunk) of Wisconsin stayed in the Northeast.

After Europeans arrived in North America, Northeast Indians' lives changed drastically. Many died due to disease and warfare. Over time, the new nation of the United States pressured Northeast Indians to sell much of their land. The United States even forced some peoples to move west. A few groups lost so many members that they no longer existed as nations. But most Northeast peoples survived their hardships. Modern Northeast Indians continue to live throughout the Northeast.

CHAPTER 1

A RICH AND VARIED LAND

The high Appalachian Mountains run through the central Northeast. Lush forests and rolling hills cover much of the region. The Northeast also contains many rivers and freshwater lakes. The largest inland bodies of water are the five Great Lakes to the west. The Atlantic Ocean lies to the east.

The climate in the Northeast is fairly mild. But the length of seasons varies by location. In the far north of the region, winters are long and cold. The far south experiences long, hot summers.

Food

For many generations, Northeast peoples called this resource-rich land home. People found plenty of wild plants and animals to eat. The forests were full of deer, elk, and moose. Northeast Indians hunted these large animals with spears and with bows and arrows. Some peoples, including the Ho-Chunk and the Mesquakie, traveled west to prairie lands, where they hunted great herds of bison.

Small animals also provided food. Many Northeast Indians hunted rabbits, turkeys, and other wild birds. Members of

A harpoon *(left)* was a tool the Algonquin Indians used to spear fish. The blade on the harpoon shown here is carved from a moose antler. Tuscarora Indians used snowshoes *(right)* to help them walk in snow during the winter.

northern nations such as the Micmac (MIK-mak) and Abenaki sometimes wore snowshoes on the hunt. Snowshoes helped them walk through the forest after a snowfall.

Many Northeast Indians included fish in their diet. People caught fish using hooks and nets. Some groups to the north and east, such as the Penobscot (puh-NOB-skot), fished for salmon during the spring. Fishers smoked and dried any extra fish they caught. They stored these fish to eat whenever fresh food was hard to find.

People along the Atlantic coast collected shellfish on the beach. Some, such as the Micmac, also hunted sea mammals along the coast. Sometimes, coastal people feasted upon a whale that washed ashore.

During the fall, many Northeast Indians collected wild plant foods. These included nuts, fruits, berries, and roots. For some peoples near the Great Lakes, the most important food was wild rice. Menominee women, for instance, traveled through wetlands in canoes. They hit wild rice plants with sticks called knockers to knock the grains of wild rice into their boats. In areas where maple trees grew, people collected maple sap in the spring. They made it into maple syrup and maple sugar, which they used to sweeten their food.

Most Northeast Indians added to their food supply by farming. Land along rivers had especially rich soil. In milder climates near the Atlantic coastline, some communities were able to grow two rounds of crops each year.

Perhaps the most skilled Northeast Indian farmers were the Haudenosaunee. This group includes the Cayuga, Mohawk, Oneida, Onondaga, and Seneca. Their most important crops were beans, corn, and squash. The Haudenosaunee

This illustration created by European Americans in the 1800s shows Northeast Indians preparing maple sugar from sap.

called these crops the three sisters and grew them together in the same plots. The bean vines wound up around the cornstalks. Both the vines and stalks shaded the squash plants below. This allowed the squash plants to thrive. The Haudenosaunee

COMMON FOODS OF NORTHEAST INDIAN PEOPLES

PEOPLE	FOOD	WHAT IS IT?
Haudenosaunee	Leaf bread	Bread made from corn, nuts, and berries baked in a cornhusk
Huron	Sagamite	Soup made from corn, beans, squash, and venison
Menominee	Pemmican	A traveling snack made from cornmeal, dried venison, maple sugar, and wild rice
Powhatan	Powcohiscora	A drink made from dried and ground nuts mixed with water
Narragansett	Succotash	A dish made from cooked corn and green beans, sometimes with meat added

harvested the three sisters in the fall. By carefully storing these crops, they ensured they had plenty to eat throughout the winter.

Homes

Most Algonquian-speaking peoples lived in temporary villages for much of the year. Communities traveled from place to place with the seasons. They went wherever the best food sources were at the time. For instance, in the spring, people might go to fishing sites. In the summer, they might go to hunting sites. And in the fall, they might go to the best places for gathering wild nuts or berries.

Because they spent so much time traveling, many Northeast Indians lived in wigwams (sometimes called wickiups). These dwellings were easy to build and move. A wigwam generally had a dome-shaped wooden frame. The frame was made of saplings, the trunks of young trees that were easy to bend. Over the frame, people placed mats. These mats were made from plants, sheets of bark, or animal hides, depending on what materials were easiest to find.

A wigwam usually had entrances at both ends. It also had a hole in the roof. When people lit fires inside to keep warm or cook food, the smoke escaped through this hole. Most wigwams were about 15 to 20 feet (5 to 6 meters) across. Grandparents, parents, and children usually lived together in the same wigwam. Sometimes several closely related families shared one wigwam.

Iroquoian-speaking peoples relied more on farm crops than on hunting, so they did not travel as much as other Northeast groups. They built permanent villages and lived in large wooden structures called longhouses. Each longhouse had a frame made of poles covered by bark sheets. Their lengths varied depending

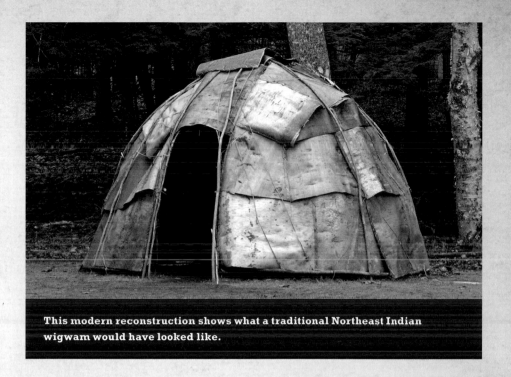
This modern reconstruction shows what a traditional Northeast Indian wigwam would have looked like.

on how many people lived in them. A longhouse could measure anywhere from 40 to 400 feet (12 to 122 m).

An average-sized longhouse was home to about ten families. Each family had its own living space along one of the house's long walls. In the middle of the longhouse was a row of fires. The families living on each side shared the fire between them. Like wigwams, longhouses had smoke holes in the ceiling.

Clothing

Northeast Indians made clothing from animal hides and furs. Men wore deerskin breechcloths. A breechcloth is a piece of leather tucked between the legs and held in place with a belt. Many men also wore deerskin shirts. Tuscarora men wore shirts made of the fibers of the hemp plant. Northeastern women wore

Micmac craftspeople made this birch bark canoe.

Many Northeast Indians traveled frequently to trade with other communities in the area. Often they traveled by canoe on rivers and lakes. The bark of birch trees was an excellent material for canoe building. Birch bark canoes were easy to make. They were also light, so people could carry them across stretches of land between bodies of water. And the canoes could move quickly through water. The Ojibwe (oh-JIB-way), Ottawa, and Menominee were well known for their swift birch bark canoes. Few birch trees grew in the southern parts of the region. So people made dugout canoes from the hollowed-out trunks of other trees. The Lenape used tulip trees, for example. Dugouts were heavier than birch bark canoes. But they were sturdy enough to travel through choppy ocean waters. They were also larger. As many as fifty people could fit in a dugout canoe.

deerskin skirts. Both men and women wore leather moccasins on their feet. In winter, they might add deerskin leggings and capes made of leather or fur. Ho-Chunk people wore robes made of bison fur to keep warm. In summer, some very young children wore nothing at all.

Northeast Indians sometimes painted their bodies, usually for specific occasions. For instance, Mohawk warriors applied red body paint before battle. Before important ceremonies, Huron men painted their faces with symbolic shapes, such as images of animals. Many people also had tattoos. Ottawa men often had tattoos of lizards, snakes, or geometric shapes that covered their whole bodies.

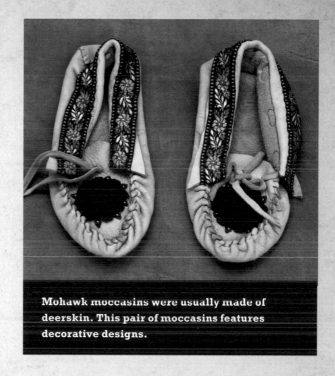

Mohawk moccasins were usually made of deerskin. This pair of moccasins features decorative designs.

Both men and women wore their hair long. They often rubbed their hair and bodies with bear grease. The grease kept their hair shiny and protected them from biting insects.

Clothes and coverings varied from nation to nation based on the environment and the local traditions. But clothing in all its forms was useful for warmth, protection, and comfort. It helped people survive in the varied lands of the Northeast.

CHAPTER 2

SOCIETY AND SPIRITUALITY

Family ties were important to American Indians of the Northeast. Whether in a wigwam or a longhouse, people often lived with their immediate relatives. Groups of families lived together in bands or villages. Most Algonquian-speaking peoples lived in bands, traveling together to hunting and gathering sites. Most Iroquoian-speaking peoples lived in more permanent villages, as did the Ho-Chunk.

A person was not just a member of a band or a village, though. He or she was also a member of a clan. Clans were made up of related families within the nation. Everyone in a clan shared a common ancestor. Many clans were named after animals. For instance, the Seneca's clans included the Beaver Clan and the Wolf Clan. Each village or band included members of several different clans.

People were assigned to a clan at birth. Among the Ho-Chunk and most Algonquian-speaking nations, children belonged to their father's clan. Among Iroquoian-speaking peoples, as well as the Lenape, children were part of their mother's clan. Everyone belonged to the same clan throughout his or her life. When a person reached marrying age, he or she usually married someone from a different clan.

Clan members provided support for one another. For instance, if a child's parents died, members of his or her clan would take care of the child. When people visited another village, they would likely stay with a family from their clan.

Leadership

Each Northeast Indian nation was made up of a collection of bands or villages. Leaders of bands and villages settled disputes and made decisions that affected their people. For example, a band leader decided when to leave a location and where to go next. Leaders often inherited their positions. But they still had to persuade their people that their decisions were good ones.

MEANINGS OF NORTHEAST INDIAN PEOPLES' NAMES

NAME	MEANING
Cayuga	People of the Great Swamp
Ho-Chunk	People of the Big Voice
Mesquakie	People of the Red Earth
Susquehannock	People of the Muddy River
Wampanoag	People of the East

Sometimes, several nations became allies and formed a confederacy. For instance, in the fifteenth century, the Abenaki, Malecite (MAL-uh-seet), Micmac, Penobscot, and Passamaquoddy (pah-suh-mah-KWOD-ee) formed the Abenaki Confederacy in what later became Maine. Together, these Algonquian-speaking peoples fought Europeans trying to take over their land. Another important confederacy united more than thirty Algonquian-speaking nations in what became Virginia. A powerful leader called Powhatan led this confederacy, which shared his name.

The most long-lasting confederacy was formed by the five nations of the Haudenosaunee: the Cayuga, Oneida, Onondaga, Mohawk, and Seneca. The confederacy was probably established around 1142. A sixth nation, the Tuscarora, joined in 1722.

The Haudenosaunee use this flag to represent the confederacy's original five nations. The symbol on the far left stands for the Seneca, known as the Keepers of the Western Door. The next symbol stands for the Cayuga. The symbol in the middle stands for the Onondaga, the Keepers of the Central Fire. The Oneida symbol comes next. The symbol on the far right is for the Mohawk, the Keepers of the Eastern Door.

Before the confederacy, members of the different Haudenosaunee nations had fought and killed one another. A Huron man called the Great Peacemaker wanted the violence to end. With the help of the skilled Onondaga speaker Hiawatha, he persuaded the nations to stop fighting and join together.

The Great Peacemaker created the Great Law of Peace, rules that governed the confederacy. A system of checks and balances kept one nation from getting too much power. Each nation in the confederacy had its own governing council. Respected women from each clan, called clan mothers, chose these council's members. Clan mothers also chose a council of fifty men to lead the whole confederacy. This Grand Council tried to make decisions for the good of all the nations in the confederacy. Many scholars believe that the confederacy partly inspired the US government system.

Religion

Northeast Indians shared many religious beliefs. They believed that a spiritual force was present in all things, including plants and animals. By performing ceremonies, they communicated with the spirit world through prayer, dance, and song.

Many peoples held celebrations when important foods were in season. Green corn ceremonies were especially common. Villages and bands held these celebrations in late summer when the corn crop ripened.

Other ceremonies differed from nation to nation. Each fall, the Lenape people held the Big House ceremony to celebrate the harvest. During this twelve-day event, people sang, danced, feasted, and gave thanks to Kishelemukong, their creator.

HANDSOME LAKE

Handsome Lake was a Seneca religious leader born around 1735. In 1799, he became very sick. During his illness, Handsome Lake had three visions. In the third vision, the Creator gave him instructions on how to live well.

These instructions became known as the Code of Handsome Lake. Handsome Lake told people to love their families, confess wrongdoings, and perform ceremonies to give thanks for good fortune. Handsome Lake's teachings formed the basis of the Longhouse Religion. Handsome Lake died in 1815, but his message lived on. Some Haudenosaunee still practice the Longhouse Religion.

About every ten years, the Huron came together for the Feast of the Dead. People dug up the bones of recently buried family members. They reburied the bones all together in a large grave. The family then held a feast to honor their dead relatives.

Medicine

Throughout the Northeast, people relied on healers to cure illnesses. They believed healers could drive away bad spirits that made people sick. Healers performed ceremonies to keep their people healthy. Among some Iroquoian nations, healers used patients' dreams to help diagnose their illnesses. Healers also made medicines from the plants that grew where they lived. For instance, the Ojibwe boiled strawberry roots to make a tea that eased stomach pains. The Tuscarora used hemp, which was plentiful in their territory, to make hundreds of medicines.

Sweat lodge ceremonies were an important part of healing for many peoples, including the Abenaki, the Lenape, and the Ojibwe. A sweat lodge was a hut where men gathered for purifying and healing rituals. A typical sweat lodge had a fireplace in the center. In one type of ceremony, men poured water over red-hot stones around the fireplace. This formed steam that caused the men to sweat. People believed they could sweat sickness out of their bodies this way.

The Ojibwe and other Great Lakes Algonquians formed a secret religious society called the Midewiwin. Its members learned how to heal the sick with medicines made from plants. They also knew special prayers and songs, which they believed helped with healing. The Ojibwe believed that the Gitche Manitou, their Creator, gave them the Midewiwin to help their people through hardships.

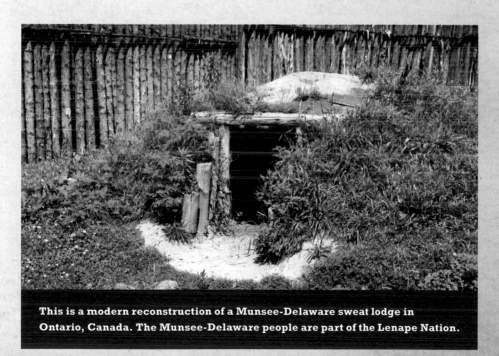

This is a modern reconstruction of a Munsee-Delaware sweat lodge in Ontario, Canada. The Munsee-Delaware people are part of the Lenape Nation.

CHAPTER 3

MAKING ART

Long ago, Northeast Indians made all the objects they used in their daily lives. By hand, they crafted all their clothing, tools, weapons, bowls, and containers. Many of these items had practical uses. For instance, where birch trees were plentiful, people used the bark to make containers. They coated some containers with pitch, a tar-like substance. Coated containers could carry water or maple sap without leaking.

But items could also be decorative and symbolic. Northeast peoples developed varied forms of art. Using materials from their different environments, they created objects that reflected their unique cultures.

Carving

With forests all around them, Northeast Indians became skilled woodcarvers. Artists carved designs into wood with tools made from bone or stone. Wooden knife handles often had decorative carvings. So did the rounded ends of wooden clubs that were used for hunting and for fighting enemies.

The Haudenosaunee were among the most skilled

This Menominee basket is decorated with dyed porcupine quills.

woodworkers in the Northeast. Their False Face ceremonial masks had carefully carved features. Many masks had twisted mouths, sideway noses, and sunken eyes. Artists sometimes attached horsetails so the masks looked as if they had hair.

Algonquian-speaking peoples living near the Great Lakes carved pipe bowls. Craftspeople often made these bowls from pipestone, a reddish stone that was easy to carve. Then a long wooden pipe stem was attached to a finished bowl. People used the pipes to smoke tobacco during ceremonies and councils.

IMPORTANT ARTS AND CRAFTS OF NORTHEAST PEOPLES

PEOPLE	ARTS AND CRAFTS
Huron	woven belts and bags moose hair embroidery
Lenape	beadwork house post carvings masks
Menominee	quillwork copper jewelry woven pouches
Narragansett	pottery masks pendants pipes
Ottawa	baskets quillwork woven mats birch bark containers

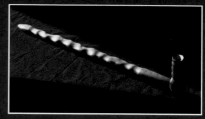
Algonquin pipe

Pequot clay pots

Menominee birch bark container and wooden spoon

Decorative Clothing

Many Northeast Indians decorated clothing with porcupine quills. First, they washed and flattened the white quills. They then colored them black, red, yellow, and blue with dyes made from vegetables. Craftspeople folded, wrapped, and sewed the dyed quills into rows to form designs.

Early Northeast Indians used shells to create pendants and decorate ceremonial clothing. Craftspeople also turned shells into wampum—small tube-shaped white and purple beads. Northeast Indians gave strings of wampum as gifts. Sometimes they wove together strings of wampum and wore them as headbands or jewelry.

Among the Haudenosaunee, wampum had special significance. People created large wampum belts to mark important events. When their leaders agreed to a treaty with other peoples, the Haudenosaunee offered a wampum belt as a gift. The belt's design recorded the basic terms of the treaty. The wampum belt showed that the leaders took the promises they had made very seriously.

New Materials, New Art Forms

When European traders arrived in the Northeast, they quickly saw how valuable wampum was. They began offering Northeast Indians beads made of glass. Northeast Indians generally did not accept these beads as a substitute for wampum. But craftspeople were excited about using glass beads to decorate clothing and other objects.

Over time, Northeast Indians largely abandoned quillwork for beadwork. Beads came in many different colors and were easy to sew into curving shapes. Colorful flower shapes became especially popular beadwork designs.

In the eighteenth century, French nuns taught Huron women to embroider with European thread. When the women ran out of thread, they turned to a material they had plenty of—moose hair. The women dyed the hair and used each strand to make a single stitch. They embroidered patterns on clothing, moccasins, and birch bark boxes.

Other items of European origin found their way into Northeastern peoples' art. Cloth ribbons became a prized decorative tool, for example. Many Northeast Indians used ribbons to create layered designs called ribbonwork. Ribbonwork was especially common among the Potawatami, the Menominee, the Ho-Chunk, and the Lenape.

Before Europeans arrived, Northeastern craftspeople mined copper from underground and made it into necklaces, pendants, and earrings. When the newcomers brought silver and iron to the region, Northeast people began using these metals to make jewelry. Metal tools were also helpful to craftspeople. For instance, the Passamaquoddy used iron blades to cut wood splints. They wove the wood splints to make baskets.

These deerskin moccasins were made by Huron craftspeople in the late 1700s or early 1800s. Moose hair embroidery adds decoration.

SHELLEY NIRO

Mohawk artist Shelley Niro *(right)* hugs her friend Anita Doron *(left)*, a Canadian film director.

Shelley Niro is a Mohawk painter, photographer, and filmmaker. She is a member of the Turtle Clan of the Six Nations Reserve in Ontario, Canada. Niro uses her art to explore what it means to be an American Indian in the modern world. Her photographs often feature herself or members of her family. In some photographs, she dresses up and poses as celebrities. Much of her work pokes fun of outdated ideas about American Indians. "Some [American Indian] people think that to be Indian, you have to do certain things," Niro has explained. "[But] I'm saying that you're Indian no matter what you do."

The blades' hard edges made it easy to slice wood thinly enough for weaving.

In modern times, many Northeast Indians are artists. Some make the same kinds of art their ancestors did. They might create beadwork designs or weave wood splint baskets. Other artists prefer newer art forms. These include painting canvases and taking photographs. Whatever kinds of art they make, they follow Northeast Indian traditions of transforming simple materials into objects of beauty.

CHAPTER 4

CHANGING
LANDSCAPE

The first Europeans to reach the shores of North America came from Scandinavia. In large ships, they arrived on the coast of Canada in about the year 1000. Centuries later, fishermen from other parts of Europe followed. Early encounters between Northeast Indians and newcomers were probably friendly. Native peoples and Europeans were eager to trade with one another.

In the 1500s and 1600s, more Europeans started coming to the Northeast. They wanted to explore the region and build permanent settlements. For instance, French explorer Samuel de Champlain founded the settlement of Quebec in Canada in 1608. Champlain claimed large parts of the Northeast for France, even though those lands were already home to Northeast Indian peoples. He developed friendly relationships with some Northeast peoples, including the Huron and Algonquin. Champlain helped them fight their enemies, the Haudenosaunee.

To the south, English, Dutch, and Swedish settlers also began arriving on coastal lands. In present-day Virginia, the English founded the settlement of Jamestown in 1607. In present-day Massachusetts, English newcomers established the colony of Plymouth in 1620.

Sickness and Struggle

Wherever Europeans traveled, they spread diseases such as smallpox and yellow fever. American Indians had never been exposed to these diseases. Their bodies had no way to fight the new sicknesses. When they became ill, they often died. In some communities, as many as nine out of ten people lost their lives.

FIRST ENCOUNTERS BETWEEN NORTHEAST INDIAN PEOPLES AND EUROPEANS

DATE	NORTHEAST PEOPLE	EUROPEANS
1497	Micmac	Italian explorers John and Sebastian Cabot (sailing for England)
1524	Lenape	Italian explorer Giovanni da Verrazzano (sailing for France)
1607	Powhatan	English explorer John Smith
1609	Mahican	English explorer Henry Hudson (sailing for the Netherlands)
1673	Illinois	French explorers Louis Joliet and Jacques Marquette

Starting in the 1600s, American Indians trapped many beavers and traded their furs to Europeans. In return, American Indians received tools and other items from Europe.

The survivors had trouble farming their fields or organizing hunts. They urgently needed to rebuild their populations. So some nations went to war with nearby nations. During the fighting, warriors took captives to adopt into their nations.

Northeast Indians' lives were further changed by the fur trade. Many Europeans wanted to trade with Northeast Indians for beaver furs. Felt hats made from beaver skins were very popular in Europe. Northeast Indians trapped beavers and exchanged the furs for guns, brass pots, metal tools, cloth, and glass beads.

But trading with Europeans created tensions among Northeast nations. Around the 1640s, the Haudenosaunee wanted to trade with the Dutch for furs. To get more furs, the Haudenosaunee invaded areas in the north and west. Northeast peoples in these territories fought back. Some, such as the Huron and the Erie, lost much of their land during the conflicts. Many peoples had to move west or join other nations. The Huron, the Kickapoo, and the Fox were among the peoples that relocated. The Erie scattered and became members of other Iroquoian nations.

Dealing with Europeans

Meanwhile, Europeans were creating permanent settlements on and near Northeast Indian lands. Many Northeast Indians grew angry that their homes were being invaded. These tensions sometimes led to war. Europeans had plenty of advanced weapons, such as guns. Northeast Indians had far fewer guns, which they could get only from Europeans. So Europeans had a big advantage in these conflicts.

The Powhatan Confederacy fought against people from the Jamestown settlement. But by 1644, the confederacy was largely defeated. The English in Massachusetts and their Narragansett allies attacked the powerful Pequot (PEE-kwot) nation in 1636. Nearly all the Pequot were killed during the conflict.

After decades of disease and war, a Wampanoag Indian leader named Metacom decided to take action in 1676. He wanted to drive the English out of Massachusetts. He persuaded several other nations to join the fight. Metacom's forces destroyed English settlements throughout southern New England. But Metacom was killed, and his army lost the war.

European settlements continued to spread farther inland. Nations in the western part of the Northeast banded together to protect their lands, much as eastern nations had. In 1763, the Ottawa leader Pontiac organized an American Indian rebellion. But he too was defeated.

PONTIAC'S CASE FOR WAR

On May 5, 1763, the Ottawa leader Pontiac addressed a large crowd. He had decided to go to war with the British in his lands. He asked the Huron and Potawatomi to join him. A Frenchman who probably witnessed the event wrote down Pontiac's words:

> We should exterminate from our land this nation, whose only [goal] is our death. . . . [The English] sell us their goods at double the price that the French made us pay. . . . When I visit the English chief, and . . . ask him for any thing for our sick, he refuses. . . . [I]t is apparent he seeks our death. We must therefore, in return, destroy them without delay. . . . There is no longer any time to lose, and when the English shall be defeated, . . . no more shall return upon our lands.

Northeast Indians were also drawn into wars by their European allies. From 1754 to 1763, the French and the British battled for control of the Northeast. Some nations, such as the Ottawa, sided with the French during this conflict.

During the American Revolution (1775–1783), some Haudenosaunee joined the British in fighting against the American colonists. When the colonists won, many Haudenosaunee fled over the new country's northern border. They started new communities in Canada.

US Treaties

The young United States immediately began making treaties with Northeast Indian nations, starting with the Lenape in

1778. Each treaty created an official relationship between two independent nations: the United States and an American Indian nation. But by this time, native peoples were weakened by many years of warfare and disease. In agreements with the US government, Northeast Indians often felt they had no choice but to give up large portions of their lands. Sometimes, Northeast peoples kept small areas called reservations. Canada also made treaties. Canadian areas that Northeast Indian nations kept were called reserves.

The Haudenosaunee and the British government signed this treaty in 1769.

Some treaties required nations to move to a reservation outside the Northeast. For instance, the Lenape and the Potawatomi had to move to Indian Territory, present-day Oklahoma. Other treaties recognized nations' rights to hunt or fish in certain areas in return for selling parts of their land. But white Americans later violated many treaty conditions. By the late 1800s, nearly all Northeast Indians had lost control over their original homelands.

CHAPTER 5

SURVIVING AND
THRIVING

By the 1900s, Northeast Indians could no longer hunt,
fish, or farm as they had in the past. Instead, they
usually worked a variety of jobs for wages. At schools run by
the US government, teachers forced American Indian students
to give up their customs and beliefs. Students were allowed to
speak only English and could be severely punished for speaking
native languages.

Many Northeast Indians lived on reservations controlled
by the US government. US officials ran these reservations. So
people could not choose their leaders or help make decisions for
their community.

The Indian Reorganization Act (IRA) of 1934 aimed to
improve the lives of people on reservations. The law set
down rules for American Indian nations to create their own
governments. These governments helped many Northeast
peoples take more control over their lives. But not all nations
accepted the new law. It required each nation to set up a
government that did not resemble the nation's traditional
government. So the Haudenosaunee voted to reject the IRA
in 1935.

By the 1960s, many Northeast Indians were working to revive old traditions. These efforts continue in the twenty-first century. This photo shows a powwow, or gathering, of many nations in Vermont.

In the 1950s and 1960s, the US government wanted to save money by shutting down reservations. The government broke many of its treaties and encouraged Northeast Indians to move from reservations to cities. Many Northeast Indians went to New York City, Boston, and Minneapolis, among other places. But they had trouble finding jobs and housing because of discrimination. They also often missed their own communities.

Northeast Indians in cities started community centers where they could spend time with other American Indians. They also began forming organizations to help all American Indian people. These groups protested the way the US government and American society treated them.

Many Ojibwe helped start the American Indian Movement (AIM). AIM called attention to problems with the US government's treatment of American Indians. For example, in 1971, AIM staged a protest in Plymouth, Massachusetts, on Thanksgiving Day. The protesters reminded people that the early English colonists of Massachusetts had been unfair to nearby American Indians. AIM helped American Indian groups around the country come together and work for shared goals.

Ongoing Efforts

Northeast Indians have continued to fight for their rights. Some have filed lawsuits to regain land illegally taken from them. Through the US court system, the Narragansett were granted 1,800 acres (728 hectares) of land in Rhode Island in 1978. The Ojibwe and the Ottawa have also won legal battles. Courts confirmed their hunting and fishing rights, which were spelled out in an 1836 treaty.

Some Northeast Indian peoples have pushed for the return of sacred objects made by their ancestors. For instance, the New York State Museum had twelve wampum belts in its collection. It gave them back to the Onondaga in 1989.

Many Northeast peoples are not recognized as American Indian nations by the US government. These groups want an official nation-to-nation relationship with the United States. After a long legal battle, the Mashantucket (mash-ahn-TUK-et) Pequot gained federal recognition in 1983. Since then, they have opened several successful businesses, including a spa, golf course, and casino in Connecticut.

Preserving the Past and Building the Future

In the twenty-first century, Northeast Indian nations run a wide variety of businesses. The Menominee manage a golf course. The Passamaquoddy own a company that makes clothes for the US military. The Ho-Chunk operate technology and green energy companies. These businesses provide jobs for local workers and make money for their nations' governments.

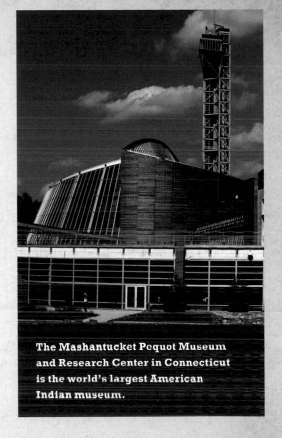

The Mashantucket Pequot Museum and Research Center in Connecticut is the world's largest American Indian museum.

Several Northeast nations also run their own museums. One of these, the Mashantucket Pequot Museum and Research Center, is the largest American Indian museum in the world. Visitors to these museums can learn about how Northeast Indians lived in the past.

Many nations are working to preserve their languages. Since the mid-1800s, no one could fluently speak the Wampanoag language. But in 1993, four Wampanoag communities in Massachusetts teamed up to create a language program. Other nations have made similar efforts. For instance, an organization on a Mohawk reserve in Ontario, Canada, offers a two-year class in the Mohawk language.

Nations also still celebrate their sporting traditions. For centuries, Great Lakes peoples have played the game of lacrosse. A Haudenosaunee team, the Iroquois Nationals, plays other lacrosse teams from around the world.

This stop sign uses both English and the Mohawk language.

Some Northeast Indian nations sponsor powwows. The Mashpee (MASH-pee) Wampanoag in Massachusetts have held an annual powwow for more than ninety years. The celebration is open to the public. It includes canoe races and dancing competitions.

In many ways, the lives of Northeast Indians are much like those of their non-American Indian neighbors. They work at similar jobs and live in similar homes. Some people live on reservations. Many more live in US cities and towns. But wherever they are, Northeast Indians remain proud of their heritage. They remember and celebrate their past. At the same time, they work to create an even better future.

NOTABLE NORTHEAST INDIANS

Eric Gansworth (Onondaga Nation)

is a poet, painter, and novelist. He wrote the young adult novel *If I Ever Get Out of Here* (2013). It is set on the Tuscarora Reservation, where he grew up.

Loretta Barrett Oden (Citizen Potawotomi Nation)

is a chef who opened the Corn Dance Café in Mishawaka, Indiana, in the 1990s. It was the first restaurant to feature dishes inspired by traditional American Indian cooking. She was also the host of the television cooking program *Seasoned with Spirit*.

Alanis Obomsawin (Abenaki Nation)

directs documentary films. Her movies depict the lives of native peoples of Canada. Her film *Trick or Treaty?* was screened at the Toronto International Film Festival in 2014.

Shannon Seneca (Mohawk Nation)

is an environmental engineer. She works to remove harmful nuclear waste that seeps into the land near her home in New York State. She also supports American Indian students who study science and engineering.

Timeline

Each Northeast Indian culture had its own way of recording history. This timeline is based on the Gregorian calendar, which Europeans brought to North America.

1142 The Mohawk, Seneca, Cayuga, Onondaga, and Oneida form the Haudenosaunee (Iroquois) Confederacy.

1607 English colonists establish Jamestown in the lands of the Powhatan peoples of modern-day Virginia.

1616–1619 Epidemic diseases from Europe kill as many as 90 percent of Northeast Indians living in present-day southern New England.

1620 English colonists establish Plymouth colony in Wampanoag territory in present-day Massachusetts.

1636 The English and their American Indian allies kill many of the Pequot people of modern-day Connecticut.

1675–1676 Wampanoag leader Metacom organizes an unsuccessful American Indian rebellion against English colonists.

1754–1763 Northeast Indian groups join the French to fight the British in the French and Indian War.

1784 The United States forces Northeast Indian groups to surrender land in modern-day Ohio.

1799 Seneca prophet Handsome Lake has visions that become the basis for the Longhouse Religion.

1830 The Indian Removal Act permits the relocations of some Northeast groups to Indian Territory (present-day Oklahoma).

1934 The Indian Reorganization Act encourages American Indian nations to create new systems of government on reservations.

1971 Ojibwe and other American Indian activists stage a Thanksgiving Day protest in Plymouth, Massachusetts.

1978 The Narragansett receive land in Rhode Island in a court settlement.

1989 The New York State Museum returns wampum belts to the Onondaga.

1998 The Mashantucket Pequot Museum and Research Center opens in Connecticut.

2014 The Iroquois Nationals come in third place at the Federation of International Lacrosse's World Lacrosse Championship.

Glossary

allies: people or groups working together toward a goal

ceremony: a spiritual celebration or event

confederacy: two or more nations that join together

hemp: a type of plant made of a tough fiber

language family: a group of similar languages

longhouse: a large multifamily house made from a pole frame covered with sheets of bark

nation: an independent group of people with a shared history, culture, and governing system

New England: a region made up of the states of Connecticut, Maine, Massachusetts, New Hampshire, Rhode Island, and Vermont

reservation: an area of land set aside by the US government for the use of an American Indian nation

scholar: a person who professionally studies a topic

thrive: to grow strong and healthy

treaty: a formal agreement between two or more nations or peoples

wampum: purple and white shell beads used as money by Northeast Indian peoples and European traders on the Atlantic coast of North America

Source Notes

29 "Shelley Niro," National Gallery of Canada, accessed April 9, 2015, http://www.gallery.ca/en/see/collections/artist.php?iartistid=24542.

34 "The Conspiracy of Pontiac and the Indian War after the Conquest of Canada," *Project Gutenberg,* accessed September 1, 2014, http://www.gutenberg.org/ebooks/39253?msq=welcome_stranger.

Selected Bibliography

Britannica Library, s.v. "Northeast Indian." Accessed September 1, 2015. http://library.eb.com/levels/referencecenter/article/117311.

Penney, David W. *North American Indian Art*. New York: Thames & Hudson, 2004.

Treuer, Anton, Karenne Wood, William W. Fitzhugh, George P. Horse Capture Sr., Theressa Lynn Fraizer, Miles R. Miller, Miranda Belarde-Lewis, and Jill Norwood. *Indian Nations of North America*. Washington, DC: National Geographic, 2010.

Waldman, Carl. *Atlas of the North American Indian*. 3rd ed. New York: Facts on File, 2009.

LERNER
SOURCE

Expand learning beyond the printed book. Download free, complementary educational resources for this book from our website, www.lerneresource.com.

Further Information

Canadian Museum of History: Woodlands & Eastern Subarctic
http://www.historymuseum.ca/cmc/exhibitions/tresors/ethno/etb0160e.shtml.
Look at photographs of tools, clothing, and other objects made by Northeast Indians of Canada.

Cunningham, Kevin, and Peter Benoit. *The Wampanoag.* New York: Children's Press, 2011. Find out more about the Wampanoag, a Northeast Indian people native to Massachusetts.

Dwyer, Helen, and Amy M. Stone. *Oneida History and Culture.* New York: Gareth Stevens, 2012. Learn more about the Oneida, one of the five original members of the Haudenosaunee Confederacy.

Gimpel, Diane Marczely. *A Timeline History of Early American Indian Peoples.* Minneapolis: Lerner Publications, 2015. Explore events that shaped the lives and histories of American Indian peoples from ancient times to European contact.

Infinity of Nations: Art and History in the Collections of the National Museum of the American Indian
http://nmai.si.edu/exhibitions/infinityofnations/woodlands.html
Click on the pictures to see objects made and used by Northeast Indians.

Iroquois Indian Museum: The Learning Longhouse
http://www.iroquoismuseum.org/virtualexhibits.htm
Visit this online exhibit to learn about Iroquois (Haudenosaunee) food, games, art, and much more.

Lenape Talking Dictionary
http://www.talk-lenape.org
This online dictionary of the Lenape language includes translations, grammar and spelling rules, and stories in English as well as Lenape.

Weitzman, David. *Skywalkers: Mohawk Ironworkers Build the City.* New York: Flash Point, 2010. Read about the Mohawk construction workers who built bridges and skyscrapers throughout the Northeast.

Index

Photo Acknowledgments

The images in this book are used with the permission of: © iStockphoto.com/Bastar (paper background); © lienkie/123RF.com (tanned hide background); © Dave Allen Photography/Collection/Thinkstock, pp. 2–3; © Laura Westlund/Independent Picture Service, pp. 4, 6; © Sean Pavone/Thinkstock, p. 7; © Marilyn Angel Wynn/Nativestock. com, pp. 11 (left), 23, 26 (top), 26 (middle); © Marilyn Angel Wynn/Nativestock Pictures/ Corbis, p. 11 (right); Cary, William De La Montagne/Library and Archives Canada, p. 12; © Kevin Shields/Alamy, p. 15; © Gary Corbett/Alamy, p. 16; © Marilyn Angel Wynn/Nativestock/Getty Images, pp. 17, 20, 25, 26 (bottom); © Daderotr/Wikimedia Commons (CC0 1.0), p. 28; © Terry Rice/Getty Images, p. 29; © Anthony Hathaway/ Dreamstime.com, p. 32; © Library of Congress/Wikimedia Commons (public domain), p. 35; Andre Jenny/Stock Connection Worldwide/Newscom, p. 37; © Franz-Marc Frei/ Corbis, p. 39; © LeeHwy500/Wikimedia Commons (CC BY-SA 3.0), p. 40; © Chris Felver/Archive Photos/Getty Images, p. 42 (top); © Larry Busacca/Getty Images, p. 42 (bottom).

Front cover: © iStockphoto.com/greatriverphotography.